AF609331

NAIJA
nah ur
MATE

PALM-WINE
PUBLISHING

Naija Nah Ur Mate
www.palmwinepublishing.com

Author - Kolade Olaiya
Book Front Cover- Kehinde Omotosho
Book Back Cover- Arts Reginald
Book Inner Formatting & Design: Chioma R. Onyekaba

Illustrations
Kehinde Omotosho
Arts Reginald
Fanen Hungwa
Daniel Enebe
Israel Obasola
Sikiru Onifade

Compiled by – Palmwine Sounds

ISBN NIGERIA- 978-978-796-521-4

NAIJA nah ur MATE

KOLADE OLAIYA

Welcome to Nigeria

Welcome to Nigeria
Where
Unemployment,
poverty, Insecurity,
etc., usually ends

By
leaving
Or
Dying

OLD NAIRA, NEW NAIRA

Listening to the radio
To take my mind off
This is more disconnected
than a zig zag line queue
that I am in, till I don't know

One of Ordinary president's guest says
The new naira is a remix of old naira
the new 200 naira looks like 10 naira,
the new 500 naira looks like 20 naira
and the new 1000 looks like 50 naira

Another guest says the new notes
Are scarce because they have
Replaced the old notes in soakaways,
Coffins, Ghana must goes, and
Bullion Vans at wrong addresses

I get to the front of the line, but
I can't buy petrol because
their P.O.S is down, and the
Supreme Court is not here
To make them take my old note.

MADAM I WANT NEW NOTES!
OGA NA MY TURN, MONEY DON ALMOST FINISH
WHERE I WON SEE AM?
YOU MEET ME HERE NAU!
P.O.S

AKWAI STRIKE

Family said Uncle is a failure
Because
he sweeps the house,
washes the cars,
trades crypto,
picks my brother,
my cousins, and I from
school, buys us popcorn,
groundnut, and ice cream,
helps us with homework.
Family said Uncle is a failure
Because
public school education is better,
Because
he has No wife,
No kids,
No house,
No Money,
and no degree
from the university,
Where he is currently
A ninth-year final year student,
That is on strike again.

Piiiiiiiiiiiiiimpiiiiiiiiiiiim
"Customer"

"Buy pure water"

"Buy Gala"

"Owerri, Aba"

Eyes moving like a compass, but it is the ears that pick up
"Lokoja, Okene, Lokoja, Okene"

In Jesus mighty name I have prayed"

"Amen"

I wear my earphones, yawn, and close my eyes after passing the pastors offering sheet of paper without contributing.

I sleep bouncing my head to Falz's rap condemning internet fraudsters
and wake up bouncing my head to 9ice's music praising fraudsters.

Man: How much is oppa
Seller: N100
Jesus is Coming Soon
The lady on Lemon is very Attractive
arts reginald
Sarah Lagos: Cant wait to see you Sugar Daddy
Man : Yes Dear
Man: Your baby is very Beautiful
Woman: Thank you

OLO'UN

The Lord protects me from insecurity when
I have 5 officers and 500 of them have one

The Lord provides me with job security when
I have two pensions and they have none

The Lord provides me a trafficless road when
I use sirens to split the road like the Red Sea

The Lord puts food on my table when,
I eat their palliatives.

CROSS OVERNIGHT

One knee off the ground before the gun shots.
Some run, some knees never get up before they drop
again.

They all cross
over.

UP NEPA

That siren sounds
makes you scream “up NEPA,”
Your fridge no longer sweats but freezes,
You put on your shirt ready to cover,
You turn off your lights, but you cannot sleep,
You wonder why some generators still hum,
Your fan no longer cools.

Inflation Nah Your Mate

Looking out the window after jamming
the door so no one would ask why I am wet,
I lower my head when I hear “buy biscuit.”

The lady behind's son cries because
she refuses to buy the shrinking gala
that costs 20 percent more than yesterday,

One of the men behind cries because it is another
month without getting paid

The driver cries because fuel costs 15 percent more
than yesterday

The other man behind cries at his stop because he
does not have money to pay,

I thanks God for the 6 km walk before the ride that
helped me afford the ride for twice as much as it costs
last week for half the distance.

There was a country

We thank God it was not us,

When the news shows corpses lined up like bush meat on a grill in a school in the north or on a farm in the south,

When the news shows suspects and guns sitting on the ground, wearing their blood and handcuffs, confessing to a kidnap,

When the news shows the mugshot of our pastor's son arrested for money laundering and BEC scams in

America,

When the news shows pictures of missing people who were kidnapped and/or murdered by the police's special anti-robbery squad,

Only to question him, when it happens to us.

In camouflage, death has a song. It can be any song, but it is usually a song with beats made from jamming hands and beating bottles and buckets.

A Hausa man chants "igbo kwenu" and swings his hands like tree branches when they answer the call of the breeze. His Igbo friend laughs at the way he pronounces the words, but dances with him.

A Yoruba man passes a stick to his Berom friend who takes two puffs before stepping on it. Although certain to win the war, they hug for what might be the last time because winning the war does not come without casualties.

WE MOVE

We waved each other bye
at work in Ibadan on Friday
after planning for the next week,

We waved each other hi
at a club in Lagos on Saturday
before sharing smokes and drinks,

We waved each other bye
In church in Ogun on Sunday
after praying for a better Nigeria,

We waved each other hi
at the airport in Canada on Monday.

Soldier Come, Soldier Go.

I watch another pile go under the soil.
An Amen and a salute will do today because
there is no liquor to push down the pain.

I put my radio on my ears and walk back and forth
towards
every direction looking for service I know I would not
find.

One moment the chirping of crickets is loudest

And the next moment the sh of the radio is loudest

I think about my mum who convinced my dad to let me join

I think about my wife. And
a son whom I have only seen on the phone.

I retire to my tent not fearing death, but anxious why it has not taken me yet.

On my birthday
I can only think about 12 days before
when for 5 hours my friend fought
to live until he bled out like a deer
even though the drunk driver was the one
who ran into him like a deer in headlights.
I can only think about 12 days before
when the Nigerian police and emergency
blew sirens for hours before they arrived
5 hours late to move my friend from one
at capacity hospital to another for an hour.

I can on only think about his mum who cries
and is consoled by family, friends, and
the family of her son's killer who want
their son to be released because
they believe God, not their son, killed her son.

HAPPY WEEKEND SIR

A plate from the capital,
A loaf of bread
Some change
A smile on their face
A smile on your face

A spare tyre?
A fire extinguisher?
A driver's license?
A kidnapper?
A terrorist?

Happy weekend sir!

WHEN WOULD WE GET IT RIGHT

Structure is not
About ideas and productivity.
Structure is,
About creating a blueprint
Where kids are out of school
and everywhere is flooded.
Not showing up for debates,
Buying crowds for campaigns,
tearing your opponent's posters,
Police tear gassing your opposition
Before your thugs beat and burn them.
About your turn to be president because
You helped install the presidents before you.

Whatagwan

The police is a man on the road
who gunshots chase into the bush.
He smokes a joint.
He stops another car for smelling like weed.

RASCLAAT!
IDIOT!
RASTA!
BOMBOCLAAT!
PARK HERE!
RASTAFARAI!
FH 11/V23

Man Must Werk

I sigh
Every morning
My father wakes up
Because
It is another day
he will carry blocks
till the sun sets
for money
to feed and
buy Panadol
for his headache
of over two weeks.

KEEPS KNOCKING (SAPA!!!)

I wish, but
I can't stop to hug my neighbours.
I cry loud enough for my passengers
not to hear me mourn my neighbours
kidnapped kids and myself because
although death is at my doorstep,
I can only hear my bills knocking.

Hallelujah Stories

I listen to men and women in suits on Sundays who make me feel like more time on my knees will make me walk on water and move mountains

I listen to men and women in suits on my earphones on Mondays to Fridays who say dreaming about making money is the way to make money.

I listen to men and women in suits once every four years debating how I will be rich as long as I sit down but once every four years to stand to vote for them.

Unknown Government

Dear Unknown Government,

We will jump out of the boot
of a Hilux with your license plate,
Carrying machetes that we will use
to sweep peaceful protestors away,

We will write you a letter
Before we release terrorists
From maximum security prisons
that don't have cctv's,

We will live in your house
When we are on the run,
And when they find us with you,
They will make you vice president

Sincerely,
Unknown Gunmen.

SUFFERATION/DOWNPRESSION

We meet our brothers in class in the U.K,
twenty years after we are born,
writing down PowerPoint presentations.

We do not sound the same, and
We also do not sound like what
Western movies think we sound like,

But, our countries leaders of yesterday
who said we are leaders of tomorrow,
are the leaders of today and tomorrow.

ABOUT THE AUTHOR

Kolade Olaiya, born in Jos, Plateau State, had his primary and secondary education in Abuja and Jos, Nigeria. He later studied at Furman University, South Carolina, USA, where he obtained his B.SC Honors in Political Science in 2017, and East Tennessee State University, Johnson City, USA, where he had his M.A. in Liberal Arts. Olaiya's poems and short stories have been published in reputable journals like Roadrunner Review, Confluence Journal, Rigorous Magazine, and Furman University's The Echo – all in the United States of America. His short story, “Facing Boarding School”, won the 2020 Excellence in Creative Writing Award. His first volume, E Be Things, which showcases his engagement with topical Nigerian issues and his concern with human rights and social justice, was published in July, 2022. Naija Nah Ur Mate is his second volume of poetry published by Palmwine Publishing.

By: Dr. Kolawole Olaiya

www.ingramcontent.com/pod-product-compliance
Ingram Content Group UK Ltd.
Pitfield, Milton Keynes, MK11 3LW, UK
UKHW021836270726
14058UKWH00002B/188